1000 DOT-TO-DOT

ICONS

Thunder Bay Press
An imprint of Printers Row Publishing Group
A division of Readerlink Distribution Services, LLC
10350 Barnes Canyon Road, Suite 100, San Diego, CA 92121
www.thunderbaybooks.com

Copyright © 2014 The Ilex Press Limited

Publisher: Alastair Campbell
Executive Publisher: Roly Allen
Creative Director: James Hollywell
Managing Editors: Nick Jones & Natalia Price-Cabrera
Commissioning Editor: Zara Larcombe
Specialist Editor: Frank Gallaugher
Assistant Editor: Rachel Silverlight
Art Director: Julie Weir
Cover Designer: Anders Hanson
Senior Production Manager: Peter Hunt

All notations of errors or omissions should be addressed to
Thunder Bay Press, Editorial Department, at the above address.
All other correspondence (author inquiries, permissions)
concerning the content of this book should be addressed to
The Ilex Press, Carmelite House, 50 Victoria Embankment,
London, EC4Y 0DZ

ISBN-13: 978-1-62686-065-0
ISBN-10: 1-62686-065-3

Color Origination by Ivy Press Reprographics

Printed in China

19 18 17 16 15 5 6 7 8 9

THOMAS PAVITTE

1000 DOT-TO-DOT

ICONS

THUNDER BAY
P · R · E · S · S
San Diego, California

TWENTY ICONIC PORTRAITS TO COMPLETE YOURSELF

INTRODUCTION

We all remember dot-to-dot drawings from our childhood—puzzles that kept us happy and busy for a few minutes as we tried to work out what surprises were hidden in the mysterious dot patterns.

1000 Dot-to-Dot Icons revolutionizes this timeless activity, turning primitive outlines into stylish, portraits with tonal shading and expressive line work. All you need is a little patience, and you will amaze yourself with what you can create with a single line. Dot-to-dots aren't just for kids anymore!

All of the dots have been color-coded to help you keep track of your position. Each drawing will take you approximately half an hour to an hour to complete, and you will be rewarded with a genuine piece of art that you can easily remove and display. It's fun for all ages trying to guess who you are drawing as you link up the dots, and it is a perfect rainy day or holiday activity.

It's also a great way of teaching kids about the principles of drawing. Through the process of joining up the dots, they will see how the lines build up to create areas of tone and give the images a sense of depth—much more sophisticated than the usual one-dimensional dot-to-dot drawing.

TIPS

- Make sure the pen you use is not too thick; test it on the page opposite before you get started.

- Always start at number 1 and don't jump ahead or go backwards.

- The finished pieces look at their best from a distance. Stand back to really enjoy them!

- If you make a mistake by connecting the wrong numbers, don't worry, it won't ruin the final outcome. Just carefully carry on.

ABOUT THE ARTIST

Thomas Pavitte, born in New Zealand in 1985, is a graphic designer and experimental artist who often uses simple techniques to create highly complex pieces, and whose dot-to-dot pieces have been enjoyed by people all over the world. He set an unofficial world record for the most complex dot-to-dot drawing in 2011 with his version of the Mona Lisa, in 6,239 numbered dots, which took him weeks to prepare and nine hours to complete. See more of his work on his website thomasmakesstuff.com and purchase limited edition prints at his online store.

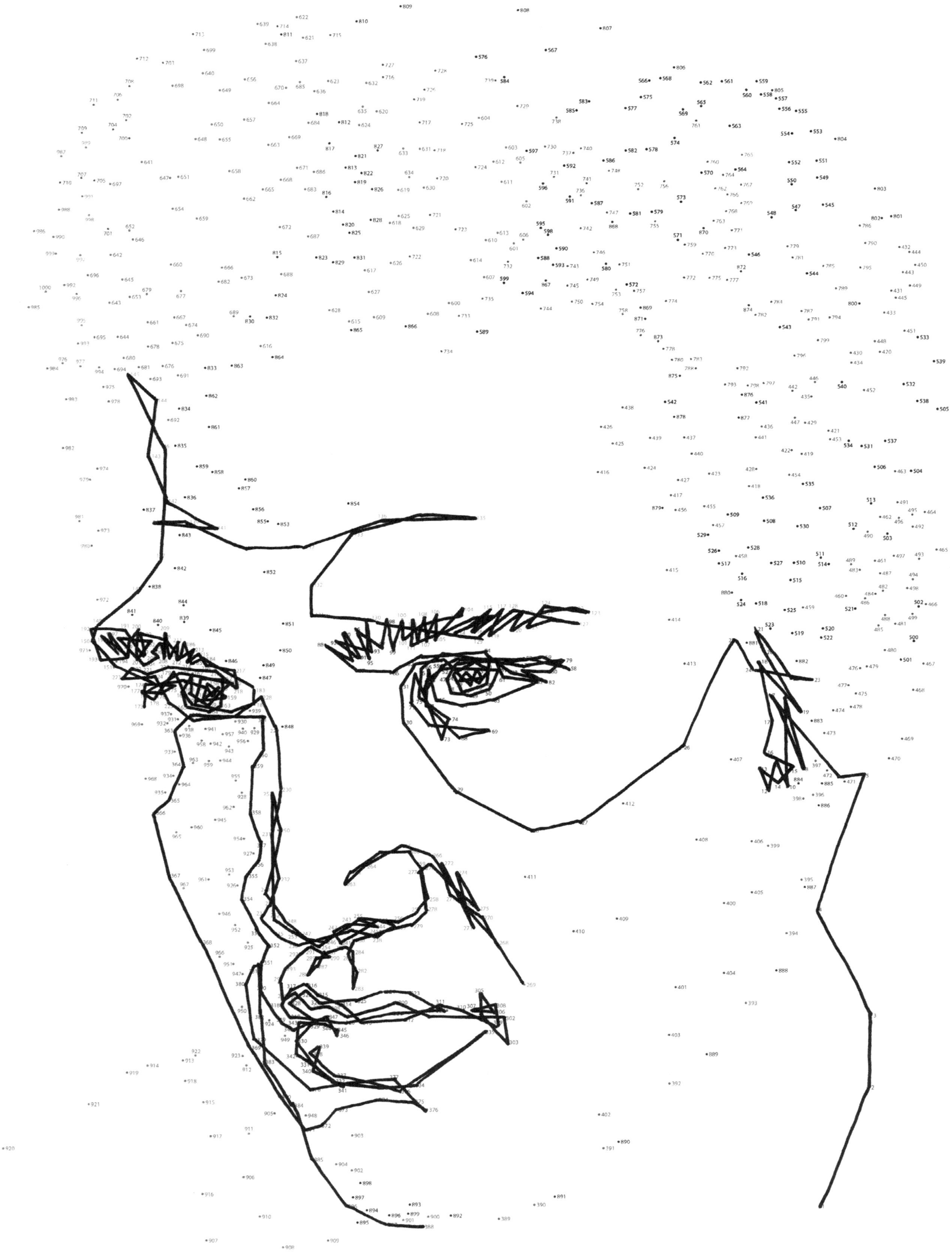

Alfred Hitchcock

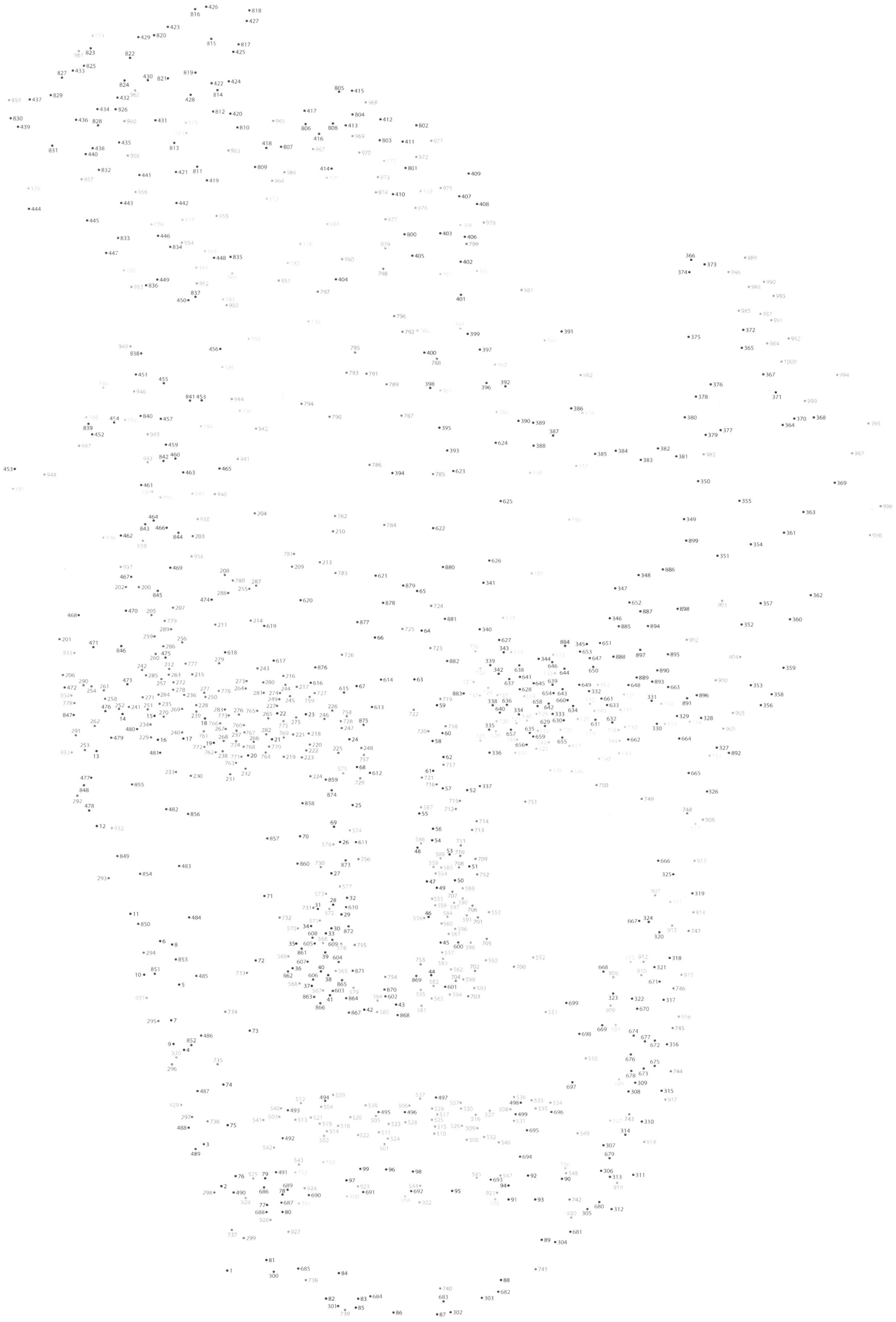

MICHAEL
JACKSON

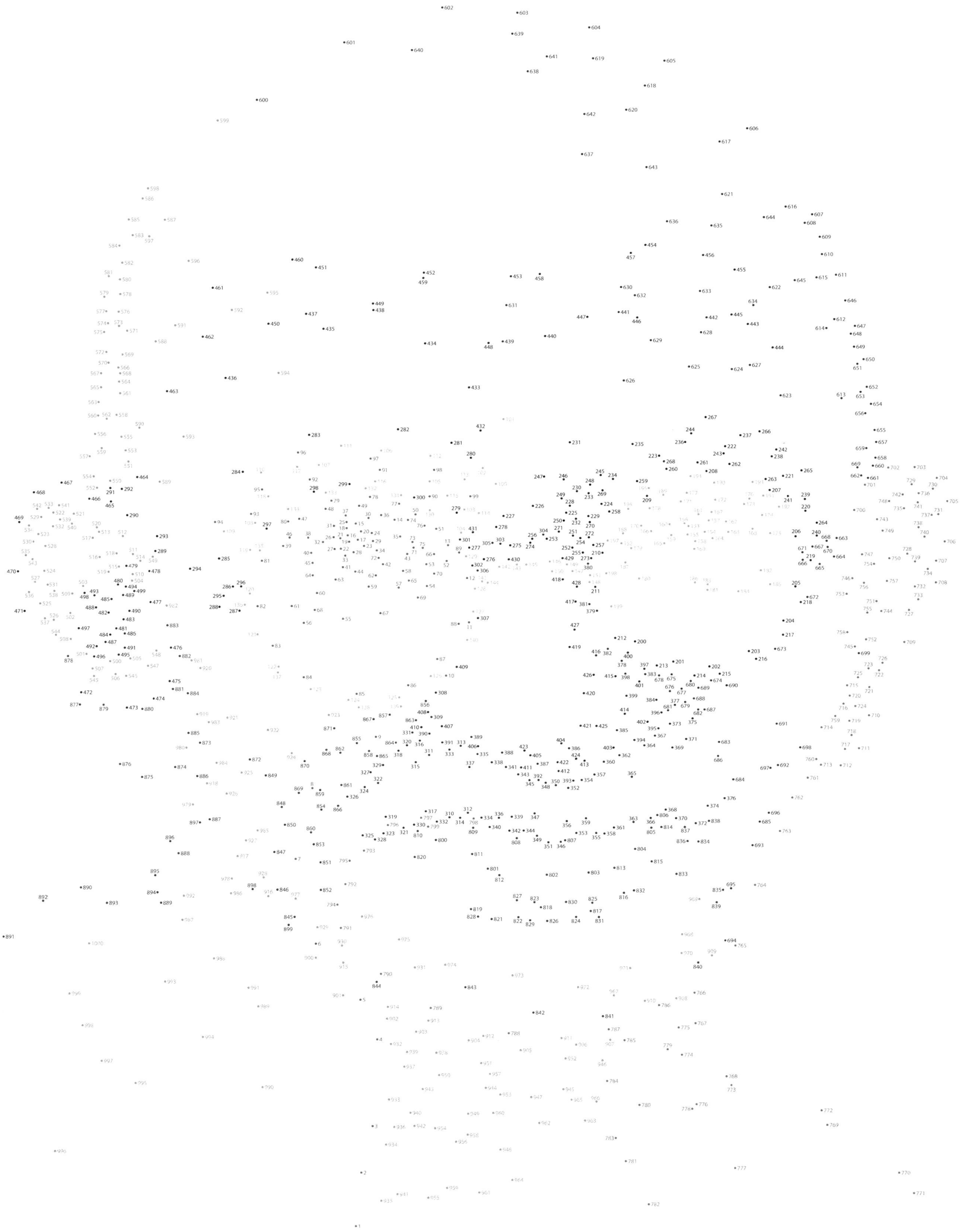

MADONNA

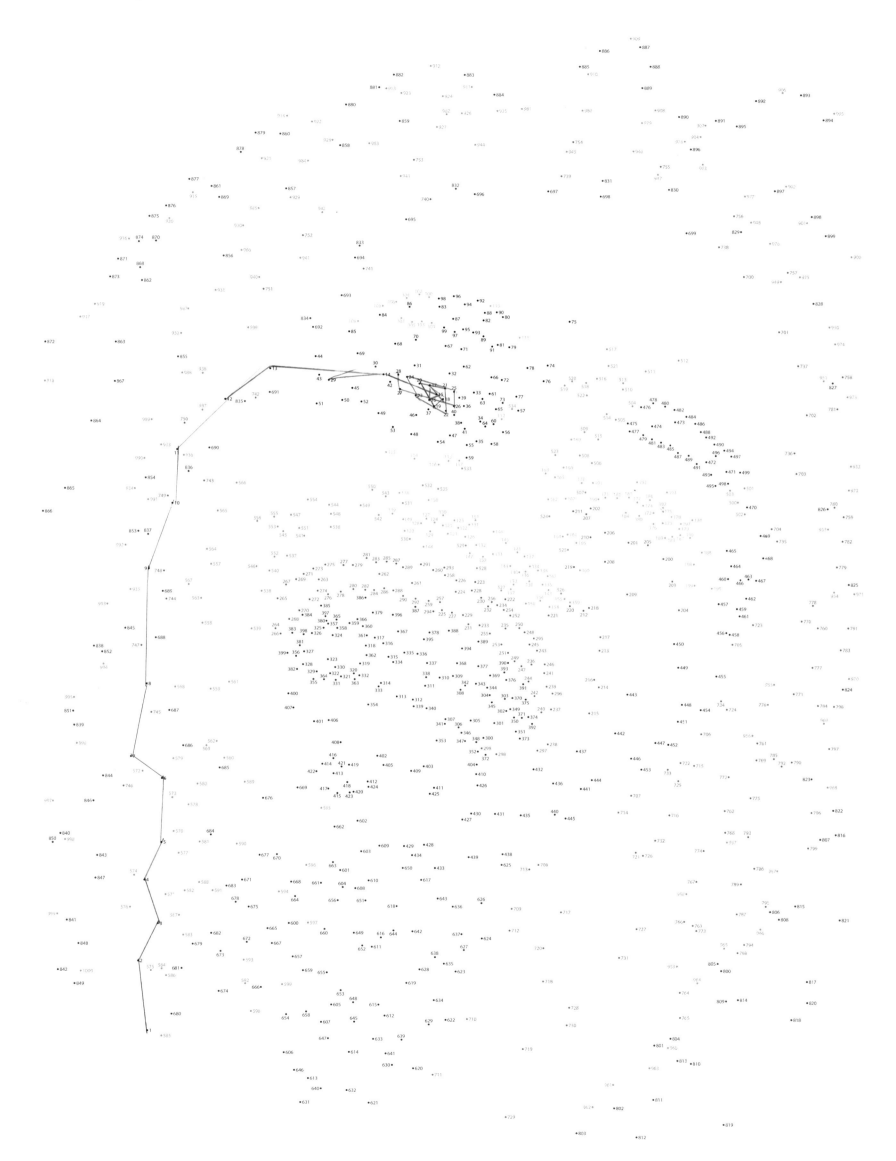

BOB
MARLEY

ELVIS

AUDREY
HEPBURN

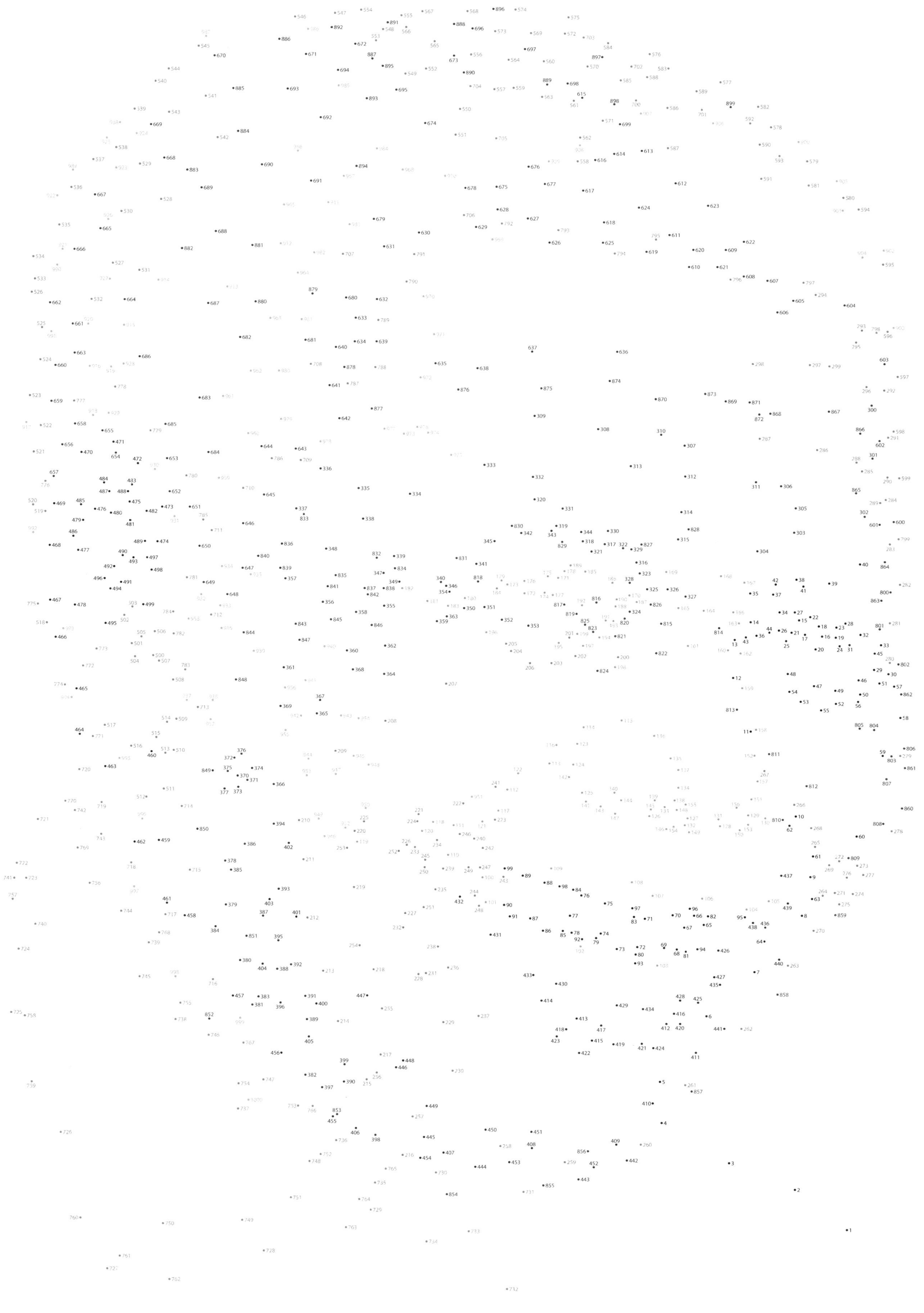

SHAKESPEARE

MARILYN
MONROE

ALFRED HITCHCOCK

ANDY WARHOL

CHARLIE CHAPLIN

JUDY GARLAND

MICHAEL JACKSON

GANDHI

MADONNA

BOB MARLEY

ELVIS

VAN GOGH

AUDREY HEPBURN

JOHN LENNON

SALVADOR DALÍ

MUHAMMAD ALI

ALBERT EINSTEIN

NELSON MANDELA

MONA LISA

JOHN F KENNEDY

SHAKESPEARE

MARILYN MONROE

ACKNOWLEDGMENTS

It has been a dream of mine to have a book published and I couldn't have done it without the support of many people in my life. Firstly, thank you to Mary and Ray for being the most supportive parents, for believing in me and for your love. And thank you to everyone else who has inspired, taught, and encouraged me along the way, including friends, family, teachers, lecturers, and colleagues, and my wonderful girlfriend, Jasmine.